POLITICS IN ONE LESSON

Kyrel Zantonavitch

TO FRANK.

Ky " Zan "

This book is printed in large, wide type -- as all reading
material should be. Most myopia in the world today
is caused by reading small, thin type.

Compliments, criticisms, comments, questions, and
detected typos are welcome. Please send them to
KyrelZ@gmx.com.

ISBN 9798452106265

* * *

Time to start a world-wide, pro-liberty revolution.

To All Good People
Who Seek Freedom from Attack
Upon Your Person and Property

CONTENTS

INTRODUCTION

Politics is an easy subject to master. You can learn it in just a few hours. And once you know it, you know it forever.

There's never going to be any more material to cover, and you're never going to change your mind about anything. Once you understand it, politics is a problem solved – permanently.

This is so in large part because political science *is* a science and is a matter of fact – not opinion. So if anyone ever holds a political "opinion" about something, then he's wrong, and needs to learn the facts. Unlike epistemology, metaphysics, ethics, esthetics, and spirituality, political science is *not* a challenging subject-matter. It possesses no complexity, trickiness, subtlety, or nuance.

Politics began about 5300 years ago in Sumeria, or modern day Iraq. The ancient Sumerians invented government, law, and political science. And these were *great* inventions.

Governmental society is far better organized than tribal society. Under government, life becomes more civilized, social harmony increases, the culture enriches, personal greatness and happiness rises, and the individual becomes more free. These are not small things.

Still, the purpose of government wasn't fully realized back then. And now, 5300 years later, it still isn't.

This is astonishing. It defies rational belief and comprehension. Yet here we are.

The purpose of government is freedom. It exists to provide liberty to every individual in society. That's it.

But you could also rephrase that to say the state was created to provide justice for all. Or to uphold the rights of man. Or to defend Nature-given individual rights. Or to protect people and property.

There are a lot of synonyms for freedom. But there are not a lot of reasons why man hasn't achieved it in all this time.

This book attempts to rectify that. It doesn't seem to be a hard job. And yet mankind has failed for 53 centuries now, so who knows?

Maybe there's more to the subject-matter than meets the eye. But if so, I'm unaware of it. And I evidently know more about politics than anyone else on the face of the earth or the history of man.

Political science certainly *seems* to be an easy subject to master. Not a single important part of it is anything other than childishly simple. Not a single significant aspect is anything other than obvious and clear.

This brief book attempts to teach you everything – but absolutely everything – that you need to know about politics. 5300 years of mankind wandering around in the dark is enough.

Kyrel Zantonavitch
New York City
October 2021

LIBERTY

Freedom is the beginning, ending, middle, and totality of politics. Individual liberty is the essence, purpose, standard, and goal of political science. Freedom is absolutely everything. Nothing else in politics, government, and the law is important, or even much relevant, to society, economics, culture, civilization, and the individual. No other value, concept, idea, or ideal even exists!

Freedom can be described as the politics, government, and law of liberty, justice, and individual rights. These three mean the exact same thing in socio-economics and political science.

Individual liberty is perhaps best defined as the right to think, say, and do anything, but absolutely anything, that the individual wishes, provided that he respects the equal and concomitant right of his fellow man to think, say, and do anything, but absolutely anything, which he wishes. It's understood that none of these rights clash, conflict, compete, or contradict. Rather, all of them supplement, compliment, coincide, and reinforce.

For the individual this means he may neither inflict nor suffer (physical) force or (financial) fraud. For the government this means it may not engage in personal, social, or economic taxation – which would be robbery – nor regulation – which would be coercion.

For all people at all times, no inter-personal aggression, unprovoked attacks, or initiation of force is allowed. Force is only acceptable in competent, adult, human affairs when it's in retaliation against a force-initiator – and even then it must be proportionate and just. It must be socially moral and rationally justifiable.

The fundamental rights of man are life, liberty, property, and privacy. No individual, group, nation, or government can ever rightfully trespass upon them. Like all rights, these are untouchable and infinite.

Freedom can be described and defined as pure political liberalism. Or else 100% socio-personal libertarianism mixed with 100% economic laissez-faire capitalism. Both of these imply, entail, and largely duplicate the other.

To get around the problem of (coercive) taxation, and how to freely, legitimately, and non-criminally fund the government, all individuals over 18-years-old or so, in a proper, moral, and voluntary society, must personally sign the liberal constitution, and agree to abide by it, and pay some tiny income "tax", or net worth fee, or both. Anyone who refuses to sign, or doesn't pay a fee for government services rendered, gets deported and loses his citizenship. Or, at the least, his person and property are no longer necessarily protected by the police and military. But for this one-person-country, free-rider, or anarchist, there's no other penalties, including fines, property confiscation, or jail time.

All individuals at all times are completely governed by Natural Law. This is so whether they know it or not, and whether they agree with it or not. Father Reality, Mother Nature, human social nature, human personal nature, metaphysical and existential human equality, and human liberty impose Natural Law upon all men at all times absolutely.

And ignorance of this law is no excuse. Human law or "positive" law or tyrannical law never supersedes Natural Law. This universal and uniform law of "liberty and justice for all" allows for no second class citizenships, or above-the-law statuses, among the various mentally-sound, physically-adult citizens of the world.

It must be noted that individual freedom absolutely supersedes the values and ideals of democracy, republicanism, autonomy, constitutionalism, and the separation of powers with their concomitant checks and balances. All of these are merely methods for gaining and maintaining liberty. But they aren't individual liberty themselves, nor are they especially valuable in and of themselves. These political techniques for governance are virtually trivial and almost useless next to the great socio-economic desideratum of personal freedom.

Even a society governed by exceptionally foreign space aliens, who call themselves kings or emperors, and who are elitist aristocrats which pass on their rule via primogeniture, and who never hold elections, nor consult the peoples' delegates in their rule, and who have no constitution, and which combine all executive, legislative, and judicial powers into one branch of government, etc. can still create political perfection and socio-economic utopia if they have utterly untrammeled, unlimited, unchecked, fully-guaranteed individual rights.

"Minority rights" aren't real and aren't needed since they're superseded by individual rights. These are far stronger and are the only rights which actually exist. No majority (Bolshevik) or group (collective) rights exist to conflict with, oppose, oppress, or tyrannize the minority or the one.

The cynosure of government – like the locus of society – is the Holy Individual. The purpose of government is to achieve the individual good. Under no circumstances should the government focus on, or even consider, "the general welfare", "the common good", "the public good", "the good of all", or "the greatest good of the greatest number". These are collectivist, communist, and totalitarian values, notions, standards, goals, and ideals. These are utter nonsense.

Only the Sacred Self matters, when it comes to politics, government, and the law. Only the self truly exists. The purpose of government is to preserve, protect, and defend the exceptionally vulnerable One.

The "police power" of government to control and regulate society for the general health, welfare, benefit, prosperity, harmony, and progress of all doesn't exist. This illegitimate, improper, invented, tyrannical power invariably tends to create a police state. And this view of the five-millennium-old "police power" of the state doesn't represent a poverty of imagination, or some limited and crabbed view of government or society, but rather the intrinsic, ineluctable nature of the state.

Government was created to protect people and property. That's all it properly, morally, legally does.

Government by its nature is inherently reactionary, negative, and destructive. It properly forbids, attacks, and punishes crime and tyranny. But it can and should do nothing positive or pro-active. Any attempt at this will inevitably end up terrorizing, attacking, enslaving, and destroying the individual and the world.

All creative, inventive, imaginative acts by an activist government are necessarily criminal and tyrannical. A free, good, proper, legitimate government only protects and defends the individual and his rights. It protects and defends liberty and justice for all. But it initiates nothing. Such is the nature of the state.

Altho' it isn't at all politically correct, multicultural, inclusive, diverse, sensitive, egalitarian, minority supremacist, or even democratic and peaceful, freedom absolutely includes the right to be hateful, bigoted, stupid, and evil toward your fellow man, even if it profoundly hurts yourself, and all of society too. These four vices are socially and personally immoral, but they are also the individual's absolute, utter, limitless right.

Government was invented about 5300 years ago in Mesopotamia. So was writing, history, civilization, nations, war, racism, kings, priests, irrigation, the wheel, and the city. It could be referred to as the Governmental Revolution. And perhaps no event was ever more important and profound – except the invention of reason, science, philosophy, and liberty 2700 years after.

America's Founding Fathers were the greatest political geniuses and saints that ever lived and exercised power. But they were far from perfect. They debated lengthily and passionately how to balance (individual) liberty with (social) power – and never once came up with the right formula. The correct answer and recipe is: individual liberty: 100%; government control of, and social power over, the individual: 0%.

So now politics is a problem solved. There's essentially nothing more to discuss – ever.

Or at least nothing serious. Nothing important. From now on it's all an argument about president vs. prime minister, bicameral vs. unicameral legislatures, appointed or elected judges, two 4-year terms or one 7-year term for the chief executive, etc. But nothing fundamental. The nature and function of government is a problem solved forever.

And please note: Humans and state officials don't have to be "angels" to create and maintain political perfection as America's constitutional framers pitifully longed for. Neither the citizens nor the government leaders. The whole society can consist of, and be run by, Hitlers, Stalins, and Khomeinis. And you can still create Paradise on Earth.

All you need is infinite freedom for the individual. Once you have 100% personal liberty and 100% self-responsibility this will free and force the fascists, communists, and Moslems to completely behave personally, and entirely get along socially.

Individual liberty is the alpha and omega of society and the state. When it comes to political science and government, freedom is perfection, utopia, and the definitive last word.

TODAY'S POLITICAL SOLUTIONS
IN A NUTSHELL

1) Promote liberty – not democracy.
2) Promote justice – not peace.
3) Cut spending – don't cut taxes.
4) Cut regulation – don't cut taxes.
5) Simplify taxes – don't cut taxes.
6) Make taxes contractual and voluntary – and use them to defend freedom and justice, by funding only the military, police, courts, prisons, and a handful of administrators.

WELFARE STATISM

The basic idea behind the Welfare State is people are too stupid and evil to live their lives decently or properly on their own, so they need to be *forced* to do so by a wise and virtuous semi-tyrannical government. Most or all people, it seems, are naturally or inherently incompetent to live their lives correctly. So a semi-dictatorship is necessary to help out.

According to this logic, people are too stupid and evil to decently or properly prepare for their old age: to save for retirement and medical expenses, or locate family and friends to assist them on these. So, in American terms, they're *forced* to prepare via participation in Social Security and Medicare. People are also too stupid and evil to avoid excessive drug use, prostitution, gambling, etc. Thus they're *forced* to do so via the regulation or criminalization of these normal, common, peaceable behaviors. People are too stupid and evil to modestly give to charity, occasionally help out their neighbors and coworkers, and harmoniously cooperate with their fellow man. Thus they're *forced* to do so via coercive taxation for Welfare, Food Stamps, Aid to Dependent Children, SSI, Section 8, etc.

Because you, the citizen, are such a fool and lowlife, the Big Brother state – made up almost entirely of people just like you, or worse – makes many or most of the important decisions in you life *for* you. And it heavily and coercively influences you on most of the rest.

In each case, a Platonic philosopher-king or government dictator determines crucial personal decisions and pivotal life moments *for* you. You live like a child as the Nanny State orders you about and tells you how to function. This means you never grow up, never attain your full potential, never fulfill your glorious destiny, and never even become truly alive.

Thus you never experience real fun, pleasure, happiness, and ecstasy. Your sacred and irreplaceable existence is mostly ripped away from you by the semi-totalitarian Welfare State. The fullness, richness, wonder, and marvel of actual Life, and being a true Human Being, is something you never get to experience. Your potentially awe-inspiring, magnificent life, and heroic, noble soul, is still-born.

The *good* news is: you never realize what you've missed. An immense quantity and quality of life passes you by, and it never even dawns on you what you've lost. Thus you never have to deeply or truly experience the ineffable, unspeakable sadness which is your stolen and wasted existence.

Under the Welfare State, you live and die – never having lived.

THE LANGUAGE OF LIBERATION

We may need a new vocabulary for political liberty. Some of the current and accepted welfare state language – even going back over 5000 years, to Sumeria and Egypt – seems loose and awful. The very terms themselves largely aim at tyranny, evidently. Thus they likely subtly influence us, and psychologically condition us, to like and accept large aspects of political enslavement.

In particular, the words "govern" and "rule" may simply need to go. *No-one* wants to be governed or ruled by others. *No-one* wants to be controlled or compelled by the state. And "government rulers" certainly seems to imply that. Ultimately, nobody should tolerate any sort of government rule, control, or compulsion.

The legitimate purpose of government, and proper goal of our rulers, is to *protect* freedom and *defend* individual rights. Thus government should probably be called "protectment" or "defensement" or some such. Rulers should be called "protectors" or "defenders". By employing these terms, the state would be naturally less inclined to lord it over us and boss us around. More importantly, we'd be far less likely to tolerate it.

The state's dependent, or even servile, status would be more apparent. Government agents wouldn't be regarded as community "leaders". They would far more readily be seen as, and see themselves as, "public servants" or "social servers"; maybe even as societal "concierges" or "handmaiden" or "assistants" or even "go-fers". The whole atmosphere around, and attitude toward, government might radically improve.

Not all of today's political language is dreadful or naturally authoritarian. The designations "president" and "prime minister" are considerably less bad than "governor" or "ruler". A president merely *presides* over the government and some small aspects of society; a prime minister merely *ministers* to them.

The term "mayor" seems even more innocuous. Few if any dictators ever aspire to, or use, that title. Altho' the Latin root of the word is still the ominous "greater/larger" or "major/dominant".

In the end, if we all lived under (or alongside) a libertarian law-system administered by a "protectment", and guided by a freedom-fighter and supreme political officer called a "defender", we'd probably have a lot more individual liberty, with far greater justice for all. The state would be much more a protector of the rights of man and a defender of Natural Law.

So *death* to all governments and rulers! Long live a libertarian justice system and Protectment, guided by a libertarian champion of the people and Defender. Both new or reworked institutions will likely be solidly dedicated to *protecting* liberty and *defending* individual rights – and much less inclined to governing or ruling us: to commanding, compelling, or dictating to us.

SOLVING POLITICAL PROBLEMS

Virtually none of the greatest geniuses on the planet today know anything worthwhile about political science. And they are so profoundly ignorant that they are ignorant of their own ignorance. They essentially don't have a clue about anything having to do with politics, government, or the law. And this is a truly amazing thing when you realize that understanding political science these days is about as difficult as understanding double-digit addition.

Curing unemployment, inflation, pollution, and poverty these days is no more challenging than determining what "23 + 55" is. Defeating North Korea, Iran, Pakistan, Russia, and China is no harder than figuring out "60 + 37". Ending essentially all crime and making housing, education, and medical care both high-quality and dirt-cheap is no tougher than figuring out "12 + 44". Ending essentially all war, while liberating North Korea, Iran, Pakistan, Russia, and China, is like resolving "71 + 99".

The problem is that virtually everyone today, for all of their existence, has been brainwashed into welfare statism and away from personal liberty. And this is bad because believing in welfare statism is basically no different from believing in, and adhering to, fascism and socialism. The absurdity and depravity of such beliefs is effectively infinite.

Solving today's political problems – all of them – is not unlike solving the problem of personal starvation when you have someone trapped inside a gigantic, stocked-to-the-rafters, luxurious, grocery store. If the person inside the store has been indoctrinated all of his life into thinking that food is poison, then that deluded soul stuck inside that bountiful building is indeed going to starve to death. The situation is lamentable and pathetic, but that doesn't make the problem hard to solve by objective standards.

On the one hand, the person trapped inside the overstocked food store is going to have to read and understand a tiny number of

competent essays about the nature of food, poison, starvation, nu-
trition, and physical health, in order to escape his predicament. So
too virtually all of mankind today is going to have to lightly work
thru and comprehend a handful of competent essays about the
nature of politics, economics, sociology, government, freedom,
slavery, and the law, in order to escape their ghastly fate. It's ultra-
easy to do -- but humans still need to actually do it. There's no substitute for true facts and knowledge. And it's not possible for mankind to somehow make ignorance and lies substitute for them.
When it comes to political science, human beings need truth and
understanding.

The good news is that all we need to know about politics, government, and the law is that we can get to paradise and create a social
utopia with *one* simple idea or concept. Just one.

This is the principle of non-aggression. It's also known as the non-
coercion or non-initiation of force principle. Adhere to this and instant political perfection and heaven is ours.

This ideal could also be described as the political science of freedom, the sociology of voluntarist libertarianism, and the economics of laissez-faire capitalism.

But if someone prefers to hear this idea stated more elaborately
and comprehensibly, then here it is: Freedom is 100% good in
theory and freedom is 100% good in practice. Political liberty has
no flaws whatsoever. None, zero, zilch, nada, nothing nowhere
nohow. As a corollary, slavery is 100% bad in theory and 100%
bad in practice. It has no benefits whatsoever.

And that's it. Game over. Nothing more to see, folks. Politics is a
problem solved *forever*.

THE UTOPIA OF LIBERTY

When it comes to politics, economics, and sociology – as well as individual happiness and greatness – liberty is entirely and without exception good in theory, and entirely and without exception good in practice. How is it people don't understand this? Freedom, free enterprise, free trade, capitalism, laissez-faire, live-and-let-live, voluntary social cooperation, unfettered personal interaction, socio-economic libertarianism, and other such similar ideas and lofty goals are all flawless, and without conflict or contradiction, in both philosophical principle and real-world application. All are end-of-history correct and ideal, both intellectually and pragmatically. How can anyone not know this?

GOVERNMENT

Government, or defensement, is a freely created and maintained, unitary, social organization which forcefully defends the individual rights – or persons and property – of its members, or those who voluntarily subscribe to it. It exists solely to forbid, prevent, and punish the initiation of force. This group or state doesn't have a monopoly on the use of defensive force inside a given country, because defending oneself and hiring security forces are entirely legitimate activities, but the government *is* the most powerful and principle protector of the liberties and rights of its constituent members and commanders.

In the legal sense, defensement is the final authority and judge of what constitutes the proper and most efficacious protection of the freedom and persons of its subscribers or citizens. The government sometimes defends against foreign invaders, but it mostly focuses on defending its members from other members, so that all can live together in maximum cooperation, harmony, and brotherhood.

Defensement generally and best operates in a unified or contiguous geographic area known as a state or country. Its job and *raison d'être*, in general terms, is to keep social order and establish justice, based on agreed-upon, universal, written, objective, liberal laws.

The defensement is established and controlled by its members or citizens who voluntarily agree, by formal written contract, to fund its rights-protecting agents – including the police and military – and to obey and submit to its rights-protecting laws and authorities. Sufficiently out-of-control, criminal, and tyrannical governments can and should be rejected, disobeyed, replaced, overthrown, and terminated.

LIBERTY VS. EQUALITY

Individual liberty vs. coercive collective equality. This is pretty much the political and social uber-debate and story of the past 220 years. Freedom for the individual to economically and socially rise or fall, based on justice and the merits – or at least based on the fairly-reliable and relatively-fair opinions of the free market and free society – is the great political and social goal of all time. Forced non-political equality of the individual with his fellows – via some sort of allegedly-wise-and-virtuous, tyrannical, government, social mechanism – is the all-time great evil.

DESTROYER OF THE SOUL

Vice crime infantilizes us, and renders us fundamentally incapable of intellectual and moral decisions. We become stupid and evil – and thus far less healthy and happy.

When Big Brother lives a large part of our lives for us – and makes a plurality or majority of our important choices – it converts us from responsible, respectable adults into irresponsible, contemptible, untrustworthy, incompetent children. The loving, caring, helpful, fascist state changes us from the joyfully alive, to the listlessly existing. From the vibrant, excited, and pulsating, to the dull, depressed, and despairing.

When do-gooder Big Government creates victimless crimes, and forbids us to be free, and doesn't let us live our lives as we wish and choose – when the vampire Nanny State legally prohibits prostitution, narcotics, gambling, and even trans-fat and sugary soda – it converts us from the living to the dead.

JOHN STUART MILL ON THE SOCIETY VS. THE INDIVIDUAL

Individuals frequently, voluntarily, and freely come together to form societies, or temporary groups and collectives, for their own benefit. Individuals also frequently, properly, and by right leave those societies, or allow them to disintegrate, when they no longer serve their interests. Such collectives can include a small circle of friends, a hobby group, a country club, a large social organization, a mass movement, or even a nation-state. But in every instance it's the various individuals involved, acting singly, which make or break the derivative, subservient, provisional, always-temporary groups. Thus the individual is the fundamental unit, or foundation, of society. It isn't the family, or tribe, or society itself, which is most important or fundamental in human life. Every individual is a kind of special, and even priceless, jewel which needs to be respected, honored, and celebrated above all else.

Unfortunately, the philosophy, culture, lifestyle, and attitude of Enlightenment liberalism – which nourished and uplifted the Holy Individual to a previously unknown extent – was substantially in decline by the mid-1800s. This reverse in human progress was carefully analyzed by the flawed, but still powerful, liberal theorist John Stuart Mill (1806-1873). In his seminal 1859 book *On Liberty*, this philosophical and political thinker took note of the decline of philosophical and political liberalism in Western Civilization and observed that: "The tendency of all the changes taking place in the world is to strengthen the society, and diminish the power of the individual."

This wasn't just a matter of mid-1800s Western intellectualism valuing the rather-abstract, collective Society above the very-real Individual – and energetically promoting it in popular culture. It was also a matter of the government coercively imposing these false values and evil ideals. As Mill saw it: "There is also in the world at large an increasing inclination to stretch unduly the power of society over the individual, both by force of opinion and even by that of legislation."

The most powerful philosophical and political destroyers of liberalism in that era, such as Rousseau, Kant, Hegel, Marx, and Engels, were ostensibly pro-reason and pro-science, and thus against religion. But they sought a mental and psychological subjugation of the individual – placing him beneath his derivative society – which was unprecedented in the 2600-year history of philosophy and belief. It went well beyond mere monotheism, such as Christianity and Islam.

As Mill put it: "Some of these modern reformers, who have placed themselves in strongest opposition to the religions of the past, have no way been behind either churches or sects in their assertion of the right of spiritual domination."

Ultimately, the enemies of the philosophy, culture, lifestyle, and attitude of Enlightenment liberalism are: "aiming at establishing...a despotism of society over the individual surpassing anything contemplated in the political ideal of the most rigid disciplinarian among the ancient philosophers."

Stupifying

In the Game of Life, it's genuinely hard to: 1) determine the meaning and purpose of existence; 2) find work which is satisfying, and friends that are high-quality, and lovers who are long-term desirable; 3) become a billionaire; 4) paint like Michelangelo and sing like The Beatles; 5) discover and innovate like Leonardo and Edison; 6) build a warp drive and time machine; 7) achieve immortality.

However, it is *not* hard to create political perfection. It is *not* hard to set up and maintain an economic and social utopia. With the Non-Initiation of Force Principle, a child could do it.

So, the fact that humans currently don't live in this political science paradise is frustrating, exasperating, infuriating, and beyond all endurance.

How is it that people today are so shockingly good at television, computers, space ships, telescopes, organ transplants, fracking, genomes, quantum mechanics, and relativity – but can't figure out a god-damned thing when it comes to government?

Why are we seemingly permanently brainwashed into Welfare Statism and forever Stuck on Stupid?

Autonomy and Democracy

Autonomy and democracy are asinine and depraved social and political ideals. Government based upon self-rule or majority-rule is fatuous, evil, and massively failed as an institution. All such existing polities need to be ruthlessly and brutally crushed.

The only intellectually and morally correct social and political ideal is freedom. If autonomy and democracy ever clash with individual liberty, then autonomy and democracy have to give way immediately and entirely.

Individual freedom is idealistic and pragmatic perfection in all aspects of government and law. Stated more broadly, every living human being and society needs and deserves limitless freedom: untouched and unchecked liberty, justice, and individual rights for all.

All mentally competent and physically adult individuals – who aren't themselves rights-violators or freedom-tramplers – have an absolute, infinite, and sacrosanct right to live in personal, social, and economic liberty forever. No one, and no group, has even the minutest temporary right to limit another's freedom in even the tiniest and most inconsequential way.

Even if the societal or political group is a duly-constituted and fully-legitimate government, which is completely representative of the local residents, and totally controlled by a citizenship majority, this entirely benevolent and ingenious group and government still has absolutely zero right to take away any personal liberty or individual rights from anyone, at any time, under any circumstances.

Such a thing would constitute tyranny. It would be an act of immorality and criminality which would be deserving of instant and complete obliteration.

Individual freedom is sacred and limitless. It's beyond any micro-scopic possibility of local popular review, scrutiny, or emendation.

DEATH TO DEMOCRACY

Democracy is truly a moronic and slimy political value and coercive social organization principle. Why trust, and be guided by, the man in the street, when he is usually an ignorant bastard from hell? Why go along with, and be led by, a mindless, malicious, rampaging mob, when it is pretty much wrong about everything?

The basic idea behind democracy is that anything goes if a sufficiently large number of citizens like it. Tyranny isn't tyranny when the majority wants it. Totalitarianism and flagrant government immorality aren't enslaving and evil as long as they're backed by a free and fair election in which *50%-plus-one* have made a decision.

According to democratic theory, even if the majority do vote for enslavement, this is their right, and any freedom-loving minority or individual should passively submit to it.

Finally, according to today's political and social thinking, democracy can never really be that bad because so long as majority rule is assiduously practiced, the people always have an opportunity to learn from their mistakes. Democrats claim that the average Joe naturally tends to favor liberty, and thus if majority-rule is maintained in an inadvertent slave state, the voter will tend to correct his error, and thus choose a somewhat less authoritarian executive, legislature, and ruling party the next time round.

The only real flaw in the system, according to current theory, is that "the people" – who virtually all massmen and intellectuals today pretend to worship – will sometimes elect a political leadership which is so tyrannical that it *repudiates* future elections and democracy! This is a regrettable error in democratic theory – as the masses and the philosophes will sometimes admit – but there's no good way to correct it. War, revolution, and an ocean of bloodshed are occasionally or frequently required. Even Jefferson observed this. But – democracy is still massively superior to all political and social alternatives, such as monarchy, feudalism, theocracy, fascism, communism, etc.

And yet, the question arises: If democracy only *sometimes* leads to freedom, why have democracy at all? Why not skip that step and go directly to individual liberty for all? *Must* we so much worship the mindless, malicious massman – the bawling, brawling, milling, mewling mob – that massive human enslavement is a continuous political threat and our frequent reality?

CRIMINAL VOTING

Voting for conservatives or progressives is an absolute crime. It's an objective and strong violation of Natural Law. Voting for the right-wing or left-wing version of Welfare Statism is *not* an expression of free speech, nor an exercise of political rights, nor an act of democracy. It's a violation of the Rights of Man.

Natural Law commands, controls, and dominates *all* of us. It morally demands and enforces liberty and justice for all. It forbids the initiation of force against anyone. And Natural Law is far more powerful and important than usually-flawed and generally-tyrannical mere *human* law.

When someone votes, they are exercising political power. They are manifesting state authority. They are choosing and sanctioning the government – either maintaining or altering it. Thus the voters are responsible for their legally-chosen, morally-sanctioned representatives – for all those who are their elected ruling state officials.

Any evil or tyranny which these government agents engage in is essentially the fault of the specific voters who freely and willfully empowered them. It is not, somehow or other, the fault of "the system." Nor are their liberty-destroying acts the product of some unknown, mysterious thing or person. Thus it isn't legitimate, acceptable, or tolerable for the true decision-makers and responsible parties to say: "I may have voted for Candidate X – but I didn't want my freely-chosen government agent to violate people's individual *rights*. Thus *I'm* not to blame for his recent failure and tyranny."

Yes, you are. You and no-one else *but* you.

Anyone who formally and officially casts a vote for a right-wing conservative or a left-wing progressive is voting for tyranny. This is an indisputable fact. Such a person is legally and morally empowering Welfare Statist enslavement. It's as simple as that.

And any such person is also committing a crime for which he deserves to receive a lengthy jail sentence. If an ultra-powerful being were to somehow observe this felonious conduct, and note its inevitable consequences, he would have the right and sacred duty to – at a minimum – heavily fine and incarcerate the democracy-based rights-violator. None of the excuses and rationalizations offered up by the slavery-monger would be legitimate.

Voting for "the lesser evil" is still evil. Giving a moral sanction and legal authority to "the lesser enslavement" is still enslavement. The undeniable truth is: voting for tyranny is voting for tyranny.

As you destroy life on this planet, you aren't "just following orders" – you're *giving* the orders. You aren't somehow "a victim of the system" – you *are* the system. The evil-doer and perpetrator of authoritarianism on this suffering, miserable planet isn't "someone somewhere somehow" – it's *you!*

In a democracy, the voter isn't legally or morally allowed to "temporarily" vote for slavery "due to the current crisis situation and emergency". The political situation is *always* thus! And it's all because of you and people exactly like you. If you vote for liberty, things will change. This is one of the few ways to *make* them change.

The voters rule in a democracy. They *are* the government. Thus they aren't somehow legally or morally allowed to "do better next time". That's a time which will never come. And even if, based on deluded theory, the "temporary emergency" ends in some never-never land fantasy future, and thus the time to vote for freedom finally arrives, the voter is still responsible for his *current* votes and the *current* tyranny. All of the suffering and miserable people of today are still his fault.

This evil voter is guilty of, and legally responsible for, an objective violation of Natural Law in the here and now. He is an absolute criminal. He needs to be punished. He deserves to be stripped of his citizenship, severely fined, harshly beaten, imprisoned for a lengthy sentence, and then deported as an enemy alien.

For all those who claim to love liberty, as they invariably vote for Welfare Statist slavery, I say: It's time to do the ethically and practically *right* thing, for once. If not you, who? If not now, when?

For all the Objectivists out there, the undeniable, inescapable, sad fact is the world's greatest freedom-fighter, Ayn Rand, almost always supported and voted for the pro-slavery conservatives. But she was morally depraved and criminally liable for doing so. So are you.

Perhaps you – the liberty-destroying Objectivists and libertarians – are pragmatically safe in your fascist and socialist irresponsibility. Perhaps no-one will actually capture and punish you for your defense and maintenance of Welfare Statism. But the ineluctable fact is you are committing a serious felony – of your own free choice – and you *deserve* to be criminally punished.

So: Who is the political destroyer and tyrannizer of the world today? Who is the horrific free agent and inexcusable monster who is morally, legally, and criminally responsible for our current, miserable, government enslavement? You already know the answer to that. *You* are.

THROW YOUR VOTE AWAY!

Throw your vote away. Always!

Never be "practical" or "realistic". Never be "pragmatic" or "strategic". Never vote for evil or "the lesser of two evils". Never vote for tyranny.

Vote for freedom 100% of the time. Find the most economically capitalist, socially libertarian, and politically pro-freedom candidate you can – and then loudly, proudly, defiantly, aggressively *vote* for him! Cast your vote *in steel*. And be sure to pause long enough to spit in the voting monitor's eye when you do it!

Your attitude and philosophy should be: no nonsense, no bullshit, no apology, no surrender, and no retreat. Go into fullscale attack mode! Take good care that you don't regret your vote later on; take good care that months and years later you don't have to rationalize, excuse, and explain it all away.

Don't ever politically advance and morally sanction slavery. Don't you dare!

Always bear in mind that if you vote for the right-wing conservatives, or the left-wing progressives, then *they* will socio-economically prosper and politically strengthen. No-one will know or care that you secretly favor liberty. How could they? All they will see or think is you're casting your vote for welfare statist totalitarianism!

However, if you self-assertively and aggressively vote for individual rights and freedom, *everyone* will know. The conservatives and progressives will both take note – and then adjust themselves in a capitalist, libertarian, and freedomist direction. This will happen both after the current election, and during the next campaign.

The powers-that-be will work for and actively court the liberty bloc. They'll tailor their positions and beliefs towards *you*. They'll noticeably alter and uplift their whole legislative behavior.

So don't be a traitor to yourself and to mankind. Don't be a fascist or socialist monster from hell. Don't help Big Brother advance.

But if you do make the decision to perpetrate an act of political raw evil and vote for slavery – in the pathetic belief that "It's just this one time", or "It's only because this election is so damn important", and you think your one, pitiful, meaningless, impotent vote among millions will make a difference – then recognize that as a result of your volitional act the freedom groups and parties will openly decline and the slavery folks will necessarily ascend.

And who's fault will that be? *Your* fault. You need to vote for liberty now and forever and always!

If not you, who? If not now, when?

When you walk into that voting booth, try *not* to be a complete and total ignoramus and scumbag! Try *not* to be a complete and total destroyer of yourself and the world! Don't do anything but vote for **freedom**, god damn you to hell!

BALANCED BUDGET AMENDMENT

Government spending is out of control, and deficit spending is wild, pretty much all over our politically ignorant and depraved Welfare State world. Thus virtually every country needs a Constitutional Amendment which runs something like this:

> "All legislators who deliberately vote for, or accidentally experience, an unbalanced yearly budget are immediately removed from office, and permanently banned from ever serving in government, or voting again. Their pensions are revoked, and the salary previously paid them must be returned, including interest and penalties.

> "All executives which attempt to implement this unbalanced budget, and all judges which attempt to validate it, receive the same penalties. All such legislative, executive, judicial, and other supporting government agents are instantly to be jailed for ten years of hard labor in a maximum security prison.

> "The unbalanced budget itself is publicly declared unconstitutional, and immediately rendered null and void.

> "To help secure a legitimate budget, all legislators are commanded to cast at least ten votes per year in favor of significantly different versions of balanced budget spending bills, until a proper budget is passed.

> "If no budget is passed within 60 days prior to the start of the fiscal year then, insofar as possible, last year's budget is automatically renewed, but with ten percent spending cuts across the board. The failed legislators

– those who couldn't come up with a successful majority vote for a yearly budget – are terminated, jailed for one year, and permanently barred from public service."

It's understood that legislators in their sessions can declare an emergency, and then have a temporarily disbalanced or deficit budget – i.e. one with a contradiction between taxing and spending – but only for a few months at a time. By the end of the fiscal year, however, there must be a net budgetary balance, or the previous penalties apply.

If anyone doesn't like this, they need to work to create giant surpluses in the early months of the fiscal year, in order to fund their ubiquitous "national emergencies", or else learn to shut the hell up!

Attempts to balance the budget with tax increases, rather than spending cuts, should result in a ten percent salary reduction for legislators for every one percent of tax increase.

No doubt this balanced budget Constitutional Amendment will cause a tiny amount of problems – perhaps even ten or one percent of what critics will likely claim. But this obligatory financial self-discipline in government will probably solve at least twenty times as many problems as it creates. The long-term, net benefit of this balanced budget Amendment will almost certainly be quietly stunning, miraculous, and utopian.

FUNDAMENTAL AMERICAN FOREIGN POLICY

South Korea and Japan today are financially rich and scientifically advanced nations. So are Germany, Britain, France, Italy, Spain, and many others in Europe. Despite their current perceived and actual weakness, they can easily use their immense wealth and technological expertise to create extremely powerful militaries with which to defend themselves. There's absolutely no need for America to violate George Washington's and Thomas Jefferson's dictum against forming "entangling alliances" with them. There's absolutely no need for America to have military bases in their countries, and to give treaty promises to defend them at a far higher level than they can decently repay. There's absolutely no need to treat them like helpless women in a rainstorm and protectively place them under America's "nuclear umbrella".

These bases and promises embarrass and humiliate them. They make South Korea, Japan, Germany, Britain, France, etc. deeply resent, secretly resist, and openly hate America. In 1991 the Philippine Senate condemned the U.S. bases there as "a vestige of colonialism and an affront to Philippine sovereignty". As *Cato Institute* scholar John Glaser noted in 2016 "such resentment can be extreme" and "can linger for generations".

These insulting military bases and patronizing treaty promises cause these natural Western Civilization friends and allies – which share so many values and have so many common interests – to become de facto enemies and traitors to each other. This phenomenon is outrageous and absurd. And so unnecessary. The natural, normal, healthy, happy unity and harmony of the West is being decimated by it.

Moreover, these unneeded and counterproductive bases and promises emasculate South Korea, Japan, Germany, Britain, et al.

They take natural warriors and heroes, and turn them into craven weaklings and submissive sissies. They make them passive and defeatist. But if the inappropriate bases were withdrawn, and the treaties radically rewritten, then these potentially noble and respectable Western powers would almost immediately acquire a backbone. They would almost instantly grow a set of highly-beneficial testicles.

No longer would these massively superior nation-states be desperate to surrender to the first disgusting communist country or pitiful Moslem state they can find. All these Western powers would rise up mightily and become a military colossus, with an irresistible will to triumph, which the non-Western savages and barbarians would respect, fear, and fawningly tremble before. No longer would South Korea, Japan, Germany, Britain, France, and the rest be abject and impotent appeasers of evil. No longer would they be repellent and bizarre "surrender monkeys" eagerly seeking out weak and failed commie and muzzie nations to servilely bow down before and shamefully submit to.

Once these great Western nations become far more equal to America, and far more self-loving and self-respecting, then the personal friendship and military alliance between them will blossom and surge dramatically. The mutually-beneficial partnership between these relatively civilized and heroic nations will become far more stable, trustworthy, formidable, and awesome.

But it can't happen until these accursed, one-sided, dependence-creating, feminizing, infantilizing, corrupting, subverting bases and treaties are terminated. Such an act would be a psychological game-changer for the whole world. It's high time America both lets and makes her friends and allies stand on their own two feet!

IMMIGRATION

In many respects, the worldwide issue of Western and American immigration couldn't be more simple. All over the planet the ignorant, immoral, and semi-suicidal Western nations are welfare statist and democratic – not capitalist and libertarian. This makes them vulnerable to, and close to defenseless against, the last half-century's flood of non-Western, anti-Western immigrants.

The fact is that in many respects these folks are nothing more than *invaders*. They don't come to join the West, or to become part of the Western family – they essentially come to economically *rape* us. They're destructive *predators*. They're something akin to human cancers, foreign conquerors, and merciless, enemy destroyers. They illegally go where they don't belong and aren't wanted. Then they *ruin* the place. And they do so deliberately, with malice aforethought.

Apologists almost invariably claim that these immigrants are merely fleeing "oppression", or seeking "opportunity", or desperately hungering for "freedom". They know very well how to play on Western sympathies and inflict unwarranted guilt. Today's immigration defenders then quickly, brazenly say that the new residents actually make the country stronger and better. Of course, this is a throw-away line. They don't dwell on this point long or offer much evidence for it. It's too absurd.

Because the reality is these new folks seeking residency usually come from some Third World, undeveloped, uncivilized *hellhole* which is almost invariably crushed by socialism, fascism, nihilism, religion, self-sacrifice, crime, racism, sexism, barbarism, and general depravity. And they bring these values and evils with them.

To make clear: they bring their heinous, loathsome, poisonous, homeland philosophy and culture with them. Then they typically, mostly *refuse* to personally uplift themselves, socially assimilate, or learn the language. And they do so proudly and defiantly, practically spitting in the face of their new would-be friends, who they generally, openly revile.

Once inside their new nation, these supposed refugees and objects of pity – who everyone is supposed to feel sorry for, if not love – then usually, shamelessly proceed to *parasite* off the new land. They massively exploit the common resources, or go on welfare, or commit crime, or all three.

And they normally *don't* learn to love the new country and its people – or even decently respect them. Rather, they mostly continue to support socialism, fascism, nihilism, religion, self-sacrifice, crime, racism, sexism, barbarism, and general depravity. They even openly express loyalty and pride in these nightmare beliefs and values.

These "immigrants" – these socio-economic exploiters and oppressors – mostly continue to love their old country and despise the new. And they actively work to degrade and despoil the new one via cultural osmosis and political democracy.

Unfortunately, they're generally very good at this. Recent world history shows it.

And all the while these immigrants generally have the raw-bone nerve to morally condemn and socially loath their new countrymen. They even shamelessly call them "racists" and "Nazis" because the hapless, helpless, hopeless *victims* of these immigrant monsters don't fully love the new invaders, conquerors, cancers, parasites, predators, and pitiless destroyers now in their midst.

The solution to the current Western immigration crisis and controversy is remarkably simple: only high-quality people who make the country *better* should be allowed inside. Low-quality people who degrade and destroy it should be kept *out*.

THE BEST IMMIGRATION POLICY

When it comes to immigration, the ideal country – the one most noble, enlightened, powerful, dynamic, civilized, just, and free – expertly and energetically imports the good people of the world while deporting the bad ones. Those who improve the nation, such as by making it freer, richer, smarter, stronger, and better, should be allowed, encouraged, and rewarded to immigrate. Those who degrade the country, such as by making it more tyrannical, impoverished, uneducated, corrupt, weak, and sick, should be kept out. Those of this type already inside the country should be stripped of their visitor's pass, education visa, work permit, or citizenship, and then summarily kicked out. Let the residents of an outstanding country appreciate their privileged status and work to keep it!

When it comes to immigration, a special effort should also be made to acquire people of merit, talent, ambition, and potential, who work hard and well, while rarely committing crime or going on charity. The ideal society should also seek those who adequately learn the local language, adopt most of the local customs, aren't bigoted against the current residents, and quickly transfer their loyalty and love to their new nation. This ideal country should also look for those who love liberty, libertarianism, capitalism, and laissez-faire, while hating welfare statism, the Nanny State, socialism, fascism, and Big Brother. It should also favor those closely adhere to reason and science; are highly individualistic; and who are generally wealthy, young, strong, healthy, handsome, sexy, clever, unbigoted, well-educated, highly-skilled, intellectually smart, morally good, and spiritually exalted. This is a rational, logical, intelligent, sagacious, virtuous, noble immigration policy which massively benefits and wonderfully uplifts the ideal country!

HEALTH CARE FOR ALL

Everywhere on the planet today health care is considered to be a "right". Society, rich people, and medical providers are absolutely, morally *obligated* to give health care to all – especially the sick and poor – for low or no cost. State force mostly makes this happen, but arguably this is the most important job the government does.

Admittedly this paramount thing is accomplished via considerable compulsion and coercion by the Welfare State. A fair amount of people in the world and the the health care industry get pushed around, ordered about, bullied, abused, and even openly ripped off in order to accomplish this task, but – it's totally worth it.

The fact is morally-advanced government today is socially and ethically *compelled* to apply its awesome throw-weight and mega-tonnage to the problem of sick and poor people who are too foolish, imprudent, unindustrious, or unlucky to pay for their own health care needs and wants. Many persons simply aren't financially or morally perfect, so it's society's and the Welfare State's responsibility to take care of them.

This is especially true because everyone knows that Big Government has the magical power to lower health care costs and raise health care quality, and generally provide for the needs of all. After all, the Welfare State can stimulate the economy, can't it?

Everyone knows that activist states can massively manipulate and control the laws of economics and thus give the people something for nothing. It can print money and make people quite wealthy from thin air. And as many smart and good people note, the Welfare State can even considerably manipulate and control the laws of Nature. Especially human nature.

Anyone who denies this is a low-imagination, anti-social element and Enemy of the People. He's a spoilsport and killjoy who secretly wants sick and poor people to suffer in agony as he laughs maniacally at their pain while plotting for Big Business and the giant insurance companies to enslave us all.

The undebatable reality is sick and poor people truly merit free medicine, doctors, and hospitals since they struggle so much, and are the backbone of our society and economy, who do all the work. They quietly, submissively, loyally work for all the fat cats and plutocrats who mercilessly exploit and cruelly abuse them as pitiful wage slaves.

So free health care for all is the least that these noble souls and great heroes should get. No-cost health care is their absolute right. The people, the sick and needy, and the poor and working class, utterly *deserve* this.

Such is the clearly correct and wonderful ideal of today's dominant philosophy of wokism, progressivism, identity politics, cancel culture, Critical Theory, political correctness, multiculturalism, diversity, inclusion, sensitivity, non-judgmentalism, cultural relativism, egalitarianism, minority supremacism, equity, democracy, and peace.

Migrant Monsters

Third World savages now effectively rule the Western World. They've won the intellectual debate and hold the moral high ground. We need to admit it: enemy invasion is now a *right*.

Third World barbarians thruout the planet have the *right* to invade the West. There's nothing we can do to stop them. It would be immoral.

National sovereignty and borders are now illegitimate concepts. Third World, savage, enemy aliens possess an inalienable right to trespass into our private realm, occupy our nations, and exploit our material and cultural wealth. We can't say "no" to them.

As a moral *principle* they can essentially beat the hell out of us and rob us blind. They can rightfully *rape* us in every sense of the word. Legally and morally, these foreigners are in the right, just as they are superior to us overall. They can do anything they want to us.

According to the philosophy of our age, these alien outsiders are legally and morally entitled to cross into the West without visas or any sort of local permission. They can legitimately assault and decimate Western Civilization with their bestial presence. By right they may trespass, invade, rob, beat, rape, conquer, rule, and destroy.

Third World savages have full reign to live their traditional lives and do their foreign thing here. And we all know what *that* means: commit crime, go on welfare, not pay their share in taxes, degrade the culture, vote for tyranny, and generally turn Western Civilization nations into Third World hellholes, exactly like where they came from.

Those in the civilized West who seek to deny them their right to immigrate, vandalize, desecrate, dictate, and obliterate are clearly racist, nativist, xenophobic, white supremacists who support the K.K.K. and worship Hitler. We're intellectually fatuous and morally depraved bigots who no-one should listen to.

We're open and brazen fascists who *deserve* to get physically and financially hammered. All our property and rights should be systematically *stripped*.

Indeed, the lifelong, heartfelt, rightful residents of the West who built this unprecedentedly good and great civilization have *no* right to be here and should ourselves be deported. All our properties and liberties should be forfeited to the invading Third World horde, and these depraved, nihilistic, rampaging enemies should, in turn, rightfully and joyfully seek to obliterate every element of Western Civilization they encounter and exterminate every white person they meet.

Such is the clearly correct and wonderful ideal of today's dominant philosophy of wokism, progressivism, identity politics, cancel culture, critical theory, political correctness, multiculturalism, diversity, inclusion, sensitivity, non-judgmentalism, cultural relativism, egalitarianism, minority supremacism, equity, democracy, and peace.

MOSLEMS IN AMERICA

The vast majority of Moslems in America evidently support the social ideals of jihad (i.e. war) and sharia (i.e. slavery), and the vast majority of Moslems in America evidently engage in the practical act of donating time and money to jihadi and sharia charity groups (i.e. supporting and funding mass-murder and universal enslavement). So why aren't the vast majority of Moslems in America arrested, jailed, executed, or, at least, deported?

GOVERNMENT GIFTS FROM HEAVEN

Everybody wants something for nothing. But the problem is you can never actually get it. And virtually everyone quietly understands this.

Nothing is ever free and there's always a price to pay. Even if you only pay it eventually, indirectly, or secretly. And usually the price for this "free" stuff is quite high. You're almost always better off paying for it directly and honestly rather than engaging in any type of amoral, unprincipled, dispiriting, and anxiety-ridden beggary or theft.

But when it comes to *government*, people today really do pretty much think you can get something for nothing. Especially the uneducated and immoral. The average person nowadays really does generally think that the government can magically generate goods and services out of thin air, and then give them to "the people" for free. Most folks even commonly think that this is the people's "right".

And the more coercive the government, the better, people suppose. The more tyrannical the state is, the more it has the power to repeal the laws of economics, physics, and reality, they imagine. Then it can give "the people" *all sorts* of free economic benefits and windfalls.

But what an absurd and malicious belief, ultimately. The people who subscribe to such egregious political and economic nonsense really do deserve to suffer.

And yet, in an odd way, this foolish and hateful pro-government coercion view is actually right. Because it's always the more authoritarian states that offer the most goodies and booty to their avaricious citizenry. They're the ones that always feature the most "economic rights" and welfare state give-aways.

People in the 21st century really do want – and even righteously demand – free education and medical care. They want free paid vacations, sick days, and personal days. They want paid maternity leave along with no-charge day care for their children. And, of course, they fully expect free public roads, parks, libraries, fire departments, water supplies, utilities, etc.

But the problem with all this "free" stuff is you do pay for it. This happens via *taxes*. And, no, you can't cleverly steal from the rich, and make them pay your share. If you attempt it, they'll probably just make you pay double. The rich and powerful can almost always work the machinery of tyrannical government far better than you.

Still, people try. The man in the street imagines the government to be almost god-like in its power and potential benevolence. So he hopes and dreams – and then is easily deluded and duped.

The results of all this attempted robbery of the wealthy, your fellow man, and the general public, is that while you do get some "freebees" of a generally crude and ugly type, the rest of the citizenry quietly raises the costs of your taxes thru the roof. And all the stolen merchandise you get ahold of via your phony friend the government is invariably low in quality and high in cost. Now, maybe you don't *notice* this. Big Brother goes to considerable trouble to disguise this reality from you. But that's the way it is.

Had you directly and honestly paid for all this apparent government manna from the sky – utilizing your individual judgment, prudence, experience, and intelligence – you and your society would be far richer overall. The massive taxes you and everyone else ends up paying is not remotely worth it.

Ultimately, whether you know it or not, all you Big Brother-loving, "something for nothing", Welfare State beggars and thieves are getting utterly conned and totally ripped off – exactly as you deserve.

THE DEATH OF PRIVACY IN AMERICA

Evidently the United States federal government is now monitoring every American bank and financial transaction whatsoever, while tapping every phone call, and reading every email and text. Our state Overlords know our phone, electricity, t'v', and internet bills inside out, while also being aware of every book, record, or video we view or buy. And, courtesy of mobile phone location transmitters, the Surveillance State now knows practically every physical step we take, and records it all in a giant, privacy-shattering databank *forever*. You have to wonder: Does Big Brother now also know all our favorite radio and t'v' shows, plus movies and concerts, plus clubs and bars, plus porn videos and sex clubs?

Government spying on innocent American citizens currently seems to be almost without limit. It's also essentially without reason or oversight. Our personal sphere has been just about totally invaded and violated. And all of this unprecedented and fathomless evil is done to keep us "safe", and "help" us.

What's ineffably sad about all this is none of these governmental Constitution-destroyers, criminals, tyrants, and traitors are going to jail. And most Americans – mentally beaten down and spiritually crushed – actually *favor* this. Evidently the popularly accepted philosophy in the U.S. is: "Bend over and take it, slaveboys!"

If Jefferson or Madison were alive today they'd *hate* America. They'd do everything in their power to destroy her. They certainly wouldn't seek to somehow radically reform our wayward social system. Their goal would be to terminate it utterly – and start over from scratch.

On the one hand, Moslems *are* our enemy. And they're everywhere – abroad and at home. No-one can deny this.

ISIS, Al Qaida, the Taliban, Hezbollah, the Moslem Brotherhood, etc. all seek to destroy the United States, and they have allies and supporters everywhere. This includes the vast majority of America's roughly seven million Moslem citizens and permanent residents.

These guys basically *love* jihad (holy war) and sharia (legal slavery). And they ruthlessly seek to bring these Islamic political ideals to a naive and poorly self-defending America. These guys also love shahada (religious martyrdom) and taqiyya (lying about Islam). Such concepts and behaviors advance their jihadi and shariaist ideals.

America's Moslems give huge intellectual and moral support to the activists of their philosophy, while also donating billions of dollars a year to groups seeking to nuke America and commit genocide against us. All these foreign and domestic Islamics are true enemies of the American people, and they desperately need to be stopped. The federal government *should* try to prevent them from doing their Moslem thing.

But, on the other hand, the freedom-hating, freedom-eviscerating Executive, NSA, DHS, CIA, and FBI are also America's enemies. They essentially seek the termination of the American Constitution, and the institution of a fascist dictatorship, as soon as decently possible.

So the question arises: How do we balance these two monsters – the muzzies and the feds – and keep them at each others' throats, but not at ours?

There are several good answers to this, but the most important one is this: We need to recognize each side's respective natures and powers.

The fact is the Moslems of today are overwhelmingly weak. It doesn't seem so to most Americans, but they're a poor, ignorant, disorganized, and temporary menace, which mostly comes from outside. Moslems have neither the money, nor the weaponry, nor the intellectual underpinnings, nor the moral stature to mount a credible assault. They're easily defeated thru countless simple techniques, such as philosophical refutation, moral condemnation, foreign propaganda, domestic profiling, mass deportation, retaking our Mideast oil, overthrowing the Mideast dictatorships, declaring war on the jihadi groups, etc. So the enemy Moslems aren't really a problem.

But today's United States government agents are very different. They're massively strong. The American federal government is a rich, highly-informed, well-organized, and permanent menace, of seeming philosophical and moral legitimacy, which comes from within.

Both groups are virulently anti-American and wildly immoral. Both hate our freedom – what's left of it – and work hard to savage it.

But only *one* group is an immense danger to our privacy, liberty, way of life, personal greatness, and ultimate happiness. Only *one* group constitutes an existential threat.

OUR DO-GOODING DEMOCRATIC WORLD

Ours is a world of do-gooding, democratic semi-tyranny. When it comes to politics, so long as your *motivations* are to do good to your fellow man, and so long as your *methodology* is democratic-ally-approved activity, then you can tyrannize your fellow citizen pretty much without limit. The transcendent social and political values of do-gooding and democracy give you such license.

Slavery is no longer slavery, if the government is honestly trying to benefit its citizens, and this behavior is genuinely supported by a majority vote. If you are engaged in service to your brothers, and backed by an act of democracy, then you can brutally *fuck over* your fellow man essentially to infinity. Any government atrocity and limitless horror inflicted upon millions or billions of inno-cents is perfectly okay – indeed, it's quite admirable – so long as you're being faithfully altruistic and majoritarian.

So enslave and destroy away, do-gooder democrats! You're the *good* guys!

LIBERAL FOREIGN POLICY TODAY

The foreign policy of America and the West after World War Two is amazing to behold. From the Korean War, to the Vietnamese War, to the Kuwaiti Gulf War, to the Iraqi and Afghani Wars, and otherwise, Westerners, and especially Americans, love to lecture the world about the goodness and greatness of their "system". They love to pontificate to the communists, Moslems, and Third Worlders about the principles and values of glorious Western liberalism. But the fact is, Americans and Westerners promote "rationality", "individualism", "universal values", "free enterprise", and "liberty" while actually knowing very little about them.

Ultimately, America and the West are mostly pro-democracy, pro-peace, pro-stability, pro-political correctness, and pro-multiculturalism – but not pro-liberalism. Like the savages and barbarians above, America and the West still love the illiberal beliefs and ideals of religion, self-sacrifice, and collectivism. Reason and science, individualism and self-interest, and freedom and justice, in the serious senses of the terms, are little known and liked in America and the West. What is desperately needed in the world today – both inside and outside Western Civilization – is a truly *liberal* philosophical, cultural, and political revolution.

The sad, obvious truth is that the savage, barbarian, criminal, tyrannical, disgusting, monkey, insectoid Commies, Muzzies, and Turd Worldies are not the main problems and losers on the planet today. It's the phony, failed, self-hating, self-destroying Western liberals. And it's the phony, failed, weak, tepid, unfocused, unprincipled, incompetent, bozo libertarians and Objectivists too.

THE ENGINES OF PROGRESS

Think of the glory of capitalism, free enterprise, free trade, and freedom generally. Think of the concomitant marvelousness of economic, social, and personal liberty.

In the modern, magnificent world of blue-collar factories and white-collar office buildings, there is at least some important division between management and labor. Between employers and employees. Between bosses and hired hands. Between magnates/entrepreneurs and their peon/peasant workers.

But despite what virtually everybody thinks today, it's generally the owners and managers which are the true "wage-slaves"; and it's the laborers and workers which are the "exploiters" and "oppressors". This is because it's the latter which takes advantage of the brain-power and creative genius of the former, and then profiteers at their expense.

In a successful business enterprise, both contrasting groups do benefit, yes. But it's the employees who gain far more than the employers. Without their company to work at, the owners and managers could almost always easily live and thrive on their own. But by themselves the hourly laborers and workers would mostly stagnate, suffer, starve, and die.

Altho' few realize it today, it's the "selfish greedy capitalist" 1% which essentially makes the world go round. They create virtually all of the intellectual, technological, financial, and spiritual wealth of the planet. They are the mighty drivers of progress. Their ability, insight, and virtue is responsible for virtually all of the ascent of man. The "poor and working class" 99% is mostly just along for the ride. The do little but parasite off their betters.

Current Western civilization and our post-Industrial Revolution society are much more wealthy, healthy, safe, secure, comfortable, taken-care-of, pleasure-filled, and happy today than in the pre-classical, monarchical, and tribal eras. This is due to such geniuses and heroes as Aristotle, Epicurus, Cicero, and Lucretius; Locke, Smith, Voltaire, and Jefferson; Bastiat, Mises, Hayek, and Rand; Pasteur, Marconi, Pauling, and Einstein; da Vinci, Edison, Ford, and Jobs. It isn't due to "the average Joe" or "man in the street", no matter how numerous and hard-working he is.

The society, culture, and lifestyle of the West today are not better and sweeter due to "the workers" or "the people". These pretty much worthless folk basically didn't help out a bit. Indeed, these mediocrities and non-entities – if not disgusting insects and menacing predators – have mostly slowed progress down. These 99% have virtually always stood in the way of mankind rising, while still taking time out to financially, socially, personally, and spiritually rape their superiors, to whom humanity owes virtually all of our current goodness and greatness.

SELFISHNESS AND GREED

"Greed, for lack of a better word, is good. Greed is right. Greed works. Greed clarifies, cuts through, and captures the essence of the evolutionary spirit. Greed, in all of its forms – greed for life, for money, for love, knowledge – has marked the upward surge of mankind. And greed... will...save the USA." –Gordo Gekko, the film *Wall Street*, 1987

Everyone should be selfish always. Everyone should be greedy at all times. Everyone should selfishly pursue, and greedily lust after, their own greatness and happiness without limit.

Life is all about personal achievement and individual accomplishment. Life is all about pleasure and enjoyment. To be morally and spiritually good and great, one must selfishly and greedily focus on these personal standards and goals, with passion and ferocity, at all costs.

Being massively selfish and greedy is the key to prosperity and joy for both the Holy Individual and his derivative society. Anyone who cares about human pleasure and the good life for all – for a world where every Individual and all of mankind magnificently thrives – must emphatically promote the ethical guides and ideals of selfishness and greed. Nothing in the entire virtuous world yields more eudemonia for humanity than these two natural, normal, healthy, rational, wise, noble North Stars.

Such is human nature, both personal and social. Such is the normal, natural, legitimate, proper, logical, scientific, healthy, beautiful way human beings truly are and invariably should act.

It's when human beings pretend to be unselfish and sacrificing to others – or worse, actually are so – that all the problems begin in personal well-being and social harmony. The Individual and society quickly disintegrate, mutually destroy, and miserably perish.

The fact is each lone Sacred Self knows himself, and his needs and wants, the best by far. No idealized philosopher-king or ultra-ingenious-and-saintly dictator or theoretical supercomputer can ever remotely compare in the Individual's knowledge of himself. And each single Sacred Self is driven to satisfy his needs and wants the best. No paternalistic guidance or outside cajoling can minutely compare in this motivation. And each separate Sacred Self has the greatest ability to achieve his wants and needs the best. No outside entity of whatever skill and power can remotely compare to this all-important talent.

For a man to serve or self-sacrifice for his brothers, while they serve or self-sacrifice for him, is absurd. This isn't his job. This isn't any of his business. This isn't why he was put here on this earth. This "brother's keeper" monstrosity violates human nature and the nature of all of living existence. Invariably, in this ludicrous trade and stratagem, both sides lose badly.

For a person to repudiate and immolate himself for the benefit of "god" – which gives every evidence of not existing – is bizarre and crazy. Even if god does exist there's no indication whatsoever that he or it wants your servitude or will experience any type of value or pleasure in "receiving" it. If anything, god wants you to fully exploit and enjoy the one and only brief life and supreme treasure he seems to have given you.

For a person to repudiate and immolate himself for the benefit of the amorphous, indifferent, destructive "collective" – which has no independent or real values, goals, and existence – is also bizarre and crazy. However common for today and the past 2600 years, this serpentine, torturous, inefficient, and hilariously incompetent way to achieve human needs, wants, pleasures, and happiness is so irrational and foolish as to be effectively insane.

To the extent this wretched, contemptible, ugly, moral belief and ideal of unselfishness and sacrifice is actually practiced, the invariable result of altruistic servitude to "god", or the Other, or the Group, is total devastation and universal agony.

Life is sacred. Life is special and unique. And so is every human Individual inside it. The precious, priceless, sacrosanct, and untouchable Individual should be cherished and worshiped at all times and at all costs by society and the entire, elaborate, social structure. Everything whatsoever should be oriented toward Him.

Practically everybody has hopes and dreams. Practically everybody has profound values, high standards, and noble ideals. It's the sacred and absolute duty of each Individual to chase and realize them with as much selfishness and greed as humanly possible. Thus anyone and everyone who genuinely cares about the greatness and happiness of the Holy Individual, and the success of his subsequent society, needs to dedicate himself overwhelmingly and utterly to the noble and heroic moral ideal of 100% selfishness and 100% greed.

And what is the *one* societal system which supports and promotes selfishness and greed? The one based upon freedom and individual rights. The one based upon personal liberty, social libertarianism, and economic capitalism. The one properly known as *pure liberalism*.

CYBER-WARRIORS' PRIORITY ONE

I call upon all cyber-warriors in the world to fight for freedom. To defend liberty, justice, and individual rights. To preserve, protect, defend, and extend the rights of man, including to cyberspace. To uphold human rights at all times, in all places, under all circumstances, no matter what.

You are the most powerful soldiers on the face of the earth. Or you soon will be. More formidable and terrifying than the nuclear weapons commanders. Stronger and potentially more destructive than than those who directly possess and control WMDs. No-one on earth can more readily obliterate – or protect – life and liberty than you can.

The warriors of cyberspace – the destructive spies, hackers, thieves, hijackers, backdoor invaders, virus writers, malware coders, bot implanters, etc., and the heroes who defend against them – have more practical ability to do good and evil than your military brothers and rivals of land, sea, air, and space. Computer fighters are the toughest and baddest and strongest of them all.

I respectfully and politely – but emphatically and unyieldingly – request, demand, and command that *all* of you adhere to the standards and ideals of worldwide non-aggression. Of the non-initiation of force against innocents and the non-violent. This applies to whether you're investigating your own countrymen (via surveillance) or seeking to hurt foreigners and enemies (via war).

Stand up for liberty at all times! This is an *order*. It is not optional whether you will or will not comply. This command supersedes that of any government on earth – any civilian or military official or authority, no matter how high.

The good people and cyber-warriors of China, Russia, and Islam today are particularly ordered and compelled to not be national-istic, chauvinistic, tribalist, xenophobic, or loyal to some form of religion, socialism, or traditional authoritarianism. The culturally superior and currently more civilized people of America and the West are similarly so ordered.

Resist and fight slavery at all times! Do not surrender to evil. Do not support or submit to any form of tyranny. Back up your free-dom-loving brothers everywhere on earth.

Support the holy causes of self-interest, personal happiness, in-dividualism, individual rights, and universal freedom worldwide. No ethical collectivism or altruism permitted. No attacks on living for your own sake, or being an end in yourself allowed. No in-fringement of the life, liberty, property, privacy, pleasure, and tri-umph of the Sacred Self tolerated.

These are the values, standards, and ideals of good people every-where. This is what *true* patriots do, support, and ferociously fight for. They stand up for individual rights, individual responsibil-ity, individual happiness, individual greatness, and the equal and limitless right to life, liberty, property, and privacy of all.

Cyber-warriors, now and always, need to be noble fighters in the unending battle between good and evil. You need to be intransi-gent, defiant, heroic paladins in the fight for freedom. You need to be manifestly, overwhelmingly, utterly, and forever on the side of the *good*.

Protect liberty above all else. Defend freedom, justice, and individ-ual rights to the ends of the earth. This is your permanent com-mand and order for all time.

NOTE TO THE POLICE AND MILITARY

This is a special message to all the police officers and military soldiers on the planet: You must obey Natural Law at all times. You can not violate it. And ignorance of this Law is no excuse.

You must defend liberty and justice at all times. You must uphold individual rights always. This is your absolute job and sacred moral duty.

It doesn't matter what the human law is or what your orders are. The government authorities and your commanding officers can not morally or legally require you to violate the rights of man. If they do, they are criminals and tyrants. If they are, you must break those laws and violate those orders.

The rights of man are sacred and untouchable.

People and property must never be threatened or trespassed. They are holy and the very purpose of government. They are the very focus of the police and the military. You may not attack or damage people or property ever.

No matter how much your government is properly representative, fully legitimate, and completely democratic – and no matter how much the laws are "do-gooding" or "for the common good" or benevolently and wisely crafted "in the public interest" and "for the greatest good of the greatest number" – you may still never degrade or diminish individual rights. Liberty and justice for all are still commanding, overarching, and perfect standards and ideals which you may never breach – or even slightly, briefly trespass.

If some flawed human law or order, or malicious commanding officer, or dictatorial political authority tells you to violate liberty, justice, or the rights of man, it is your absolute duty and unavoidable, personal obligation to disobey. You must protect freedom always. You must preserve, protect, and defend people and property at all times and no matter what.

The highest legal and political authority on the planet is he whose knowledge of politics, government, and the law is most authoritative. That might be *me*. And so my or their standing orders are: Defend freedom always.

These orders can never be countermanded, belayed, or disobeyed. You must adhere to Natural Law at all costs. You must enforce and uphold the inherent and Nature-given rights to life, liberty, property, and privacy no matter what.

Liberty and justice for all are inalienable rights which are indelibly and undeniably written into human nature. These are some of the supreme laws of reality. You cannot violate them ever.

The protection of people and their property is the foundation of society, civilization, harmony, progress, greatness, and happiness. This is a holy thing which should never be traduced. You must protect and defend all persons and their possessions zealously. This is your standing order, permanent duty, and a fundamental law to be followed, enforced, obeyed, and ferociously adhered to under all circumstances whatsoever.

Please remember: You wear a uniform, carry a gun, and exercise political authority for one reason and one reason only: to defend the sacred and untouchable rights of man.

OBJECTIVISTS, LIBERTARIANS, AND FREEDOM

Today's Objectivists and libertarians are poor advocates for political liberty. They have all the truth in the world on their side – but they still lose pretty much every single political argument. The world at large does not come to them for answers.

Objectivists and libertarians lose the debate because they rarely employ principles or argue essentials. This book does. They don't.

Objectivists and libertarians have a hard time cutting to the chase or getting to the point – assuming they even know it. When it comes to publicly discussing the nature and role of government, Objectivists and libertarians today almost always focus on side-issues and trivia.

Rather than using their strongest weapon, and arguing the moral case for political liberty, they almost always argue the practical one. This strategy implies that virtue and idealism are on the other side, and thus undercuts them drastically.

Part of the reason Objectivists and libertarians shun moral discussion, and the righteousness of individual liberty, is they're generally uncomfortable with philosophy and abstract theory. Hence their claims are mostly devoid of intellectual rigor. They try to substitute for this with sarcasm, personal bitterness, and insults against their opponents. But serious political thinkers are not impressed.

Probably the biggest reason Objectivists and libertarians can't get across the idea that freedom is 100% good in theory and 100% good in practice – other than that they never mention it – is because they hate being hated. They quietly know how radical they are, and how much people are initially shocked and appalled at their theories, and so they assiduously avoid stating them openly or clearly.

Objectivist and libertarian revolutionaries understand how much the current political world is dominated by right-wing conservatives and left-wing progressives – and how much these two ideologies revile genuine liberty, justice, capitalism, libertarianism, laissez-faire, and individual rights. Hence they avoid mentioning them. Objectivists and libertarians can ramble on in their inept arguments for a thousand words without once mentioning them. To most people, especially the Objectivists and libertarians themselves, it seems like such a thing isn't possible. But the next time you get half a chance – take a look!

If you read or listen to what they literally say, you'll see that the "F" word and "L" word rarely or never come up. The concepts they refer to don't come up either.

Far the most common technique the Objectivists and libertarians employ, to gain popular acceptance and avoid public loathing, is to disguise themselves as conservatives. They argue – and even dress and look – just like them. They even force themselves to think like them. The end result of all this dishonesty, cowardice, and sleaze is that nowadays the Objectivists and libertarians pretty much *are* conservatives. They're widely and properly known as "people of the right" and (in American terms) as supporters of the Republicans.

All this is too sad and pitiful for words.

What needs to happen, if the Objectivists and libertarians ever want to win this intellectual battle and convince anyone of quality, is they need to finally start telling the truth. They need to clearly and emphatically admit that they reject conservatism and the Republicans – not just progressivism and the Democrats. They need to publicly confess that they favor complete freedom for every individual and thus they entirely oppose all government intervention, interference, and force-initiation in human life whatsoever.

Objectivists and libertarians need to say loudly, proudly, defiantly, and passionately:

We reject all vice laws, labor laws, professional licenses, and business permits. We reject all government charity and redistribution of wealth. We oppose all government streets, schools, hospitals, parks, transportation, banks, and money. We oppose and reject all personal, social, and economic regulation whatsoever.

Moreover, we Objectivists and libertarians think people have no right to health care, education, housing, a minimal income – or even food and water. Yes, these are great values in human life. But the free individual alone has the duty and right to seek them. And he can find them at far higher quality and lower price than with government "help" or as a "right".

Objectivists and libertarians should flatly state that government only exists to protect people and property. Hence the only legitimate government organizations are the police, military, courts, jails, and a tiny overseeing administration. Moreover they should state that taxation is theft, and thus the tiny amount of money needed to fund the government should be entirely voluntary and contractual.

They should coldly and emphatically point out that *all* regulation is criminal and tyrannical. Society and government can never regulate the personal, social, or economic behavior of man in any way whatsoever. Regulation is slavery.

Of course, the politically-pitiful Objectivists and libertarians can't really say the stuff above if they don't understand and believe it. And that's the point. They don't.

So, in simple terms, why are the Objectivists and libertarians so terrible when it comes to advocating political liberty?

First, they're wildly incompetent. Next, they're profoundly dishonest. Finally, they're extremely cowardly.

So, largely courtesy of the pathetic loser Objectivists and libertarians, the current prospects for political liberty on this planet are poor. With friends of freedom like these, who needs enemies?

POLITICS

Freedom. Liberty, justice, and individual rights. Protection of people and property. Non-initiation of force. Live and let live. The rights of man. Liberty and justice for all. Police, military, courts, jails, and tiny administration. No force, no fraud. Social libertarianism, economic capitalism, and political freedom. Laissez-faire. All persuasion, no coercion. No regulation of personal, social, or economic activity. Inalienable rights. Equal, impartial, universal justice. Freedom without limits. The right to think, say, and do as you wish, provided you allow all others the same. Sacred and untouchable human rights. Free enterprise, free trade, free association, free speech. Non-aggression principle. Individual rights. Liberty.

So so easy to understand!

Quotations from the World's Strongest Political Theorist, Ayn Rand

* If one wishes to advocate a free society – that is, capitalism – one must realize that its indispensable foundation is the principle of individual rights. If one wishes to uphold individual rights, one must realize that capitalism is the only system that can uphold and protect them.

* [T]here is no such entity as "society," since society is only a number of individual men."

* The United States [holds] that man's life is his by *right*, (which means: by moral principle and by his nature), that a right is the property of an individual, that society as such has no rights, and that the only moral purpose of a government is the protection of individual rights.

* The concept of a "right" pertains only to action – specifically, to freedom of action. It means freedom from physical compulsion, coercion or interference by other men.

* [Thus] the right to property is a right to action...it is not the right *to an object*, but to the action and the consequences of producing or earning the object. It is not a guarantee that a man *will* earn any property, but only a guarantee that he will own it if he earns it.

* The concept of individual rights is so new in human history that most men have not grasped it fully to this day... [S]ome men assert that rights are a gift of God – others, that rights are a gift of society. But, in fact, the source of rights is man's nature.

* Rights are conditions of existence required by man's nature for his proper survival. If man is to live on earth, it is *right* for him to use his mind, it is *right* to act on his own free judgment, it is *right* to work for his values and to keep the product of his work.

* The [American] Declaration of Independence laid down the principle that "to secure these rights, governments are instituted among men." This provided the only valid justification of a government and defined its only proper purpose: to protect man's rights by protecting him from physical violence.

* A civilized society is one in which physical force is banned from human relationships – in which the government, acting as a policeman, may use force *only* in retaliation and *only* against those who initiate its use.

* Any alleged "right" of one man, which necessitates the violation of the rights of another, is not and cannot be a right. No man can have a right to impose an unchosen obligation, an unrewarded duty or an involuntary servitude on another man. There can be no such thing as *"the right to enslave."*

* Observe, in this context, the intellectual precision of the Founding Fathers: they spoke of the right to *the pursuit* of happiness – *not* of the right to happiness. It means that a man has the right to take the actions he deems necessary to achieve his happiness; it does *not* mean that others must make him happy.

* Any undertaking that involves more than one man, requires the *voluntary* consent of every participant. Every one of them has the *right* to make his own decision, but none has the right to force his decision on the others.

* There is no such thing as "a right to a job" – there is only the right of free trade, that is: a man's right to take a job if another man chooses to hire him. There is no "right to a home," only the right of free trade: the right to build a home or to buy it.

* There are no "rights" of special groups, there are no "rights of farmers, of workers, of businessmen, of employees, of employers, or the old, of the young, or the unborn." There are only *the Rights of Man* – rights possessed by every individual man and by *all* men as individuals.

* [R]ights are moral principles which define and protect a man's freedom of action, but impose no obligations on other men.

* A government is the most dangerous threat to man's rights... When unlimited and unrestricted by individual rights, a government is man's deadliest enemy.

* [T]here are, in fact, no "economic rights," no "collective rights," no "public-interest rights." The term "individual rights" is a redundancy: there is no other kind of rights and no one else to possess them.

* Just as the notion that "Anything I do is right because *I* choose to do it," is not a moral principle, but a negation of morality – so the notion that "Anything society does is right because *society* chose to do it," is not a moral principle but a negation of moral principles."

* Since only an individual man can possess rights, the expression "individual rights" is a redundancy (which one has to use for purposes of clarification in today's intellectual chaos). But the expression "collective rights" is a contradiction in terms.

* A group, as such, has no rights. A man can neither acquire new rights by joining a group nor lose the rights he does possess.

* Any group that does not recognize this principle [of individual rights] is not an association, but a gang or a mob. Any doctrine of group activities that does not recognize individual rights is a doctrine of mob rule or legalized lynching.

* [T]his doctrine [of collective rights] rests on mysticism...on the social mystique of modern collectivists who see society as a super-organism, as some supernatural entity apart from and superior to the sum of its individual members.

* A nation, like any other group, is only a number of individuals and can have no rights other than the rights of its individual citizens.

* Just as an individual's right of free action does not include the right to commit crimes (that is, to violate the rights of others), so the right of a nation to determine its own form of government does not include the right to establish a slave society (that is, to legalize the enslavement of some men to others). *There is no such thing as "the right to enslave."*

* Individual rights are not subject to a public vote; a majority has no right to vote away the rights of a minority; the political function of rights is precisely to protect minorities from oppression by majorities (and the smallest minority on earth is the individual).

* A society that robs an individual of the product of his effort, or enslaves him, or attempts to limit the freedom of his mind, or compels him to act against his own rational judgment – a society that sets up a conflict between its edicts and the requirements of

man's nature – in not, strictly speaking, a society, but a mob held together by institutionalized gang-rule.

* Life on a desert island is safer than and incomparably preferable to existence in Soviet Russia or Nazi Germany.

* If men are to live together in a peaceful, productive, rational society and deal with one another to mutual benefit, they must accept the basic social principle without which no moral or civilized society is possible: the principle of individual rights.

* Man's rights can only be violated by the use of physical force. It is only by means of physical force that one man can deprive another of his life, or enslave him, or rob him, or prevent him from pursuing his own goals, or compel him to act against his own rational judgment.

* The precondition of a civilized society is the barring of physical force from social relationships – thus establishing the principle that if men wish to deal with one another, they may do so only be means of *reason*: by discussion, persuasion, and voluntary, uncoerced agreement.

* In a civilized society, force may only be used in retaliation and only against those who initiate its use. All the reasons which make the initiation of physical force an evil, make the retaliatory use of physical force a moral imperative.

* Under a proper social system, a private individual is legally free to take any action he pleases (so long as he does not violate the rights of others), while a government official is bound by law in his every official act. A private individual may do anything except that which is legally *forbidden*; a government official may do nothing except that which is legally *permitted*. This is the means of

subordinating "might" to "right." This is the American concept of "a government of laws, and not men."

* Since the protection of individual rights is the only proper purpose of a government, it is the only proper subject of legislation: all laws must be based on individual rights and aimed at their protection.

* [T]here is no such entity as "society," since society is only a number of individual men..." The proper functions of a government fall into three broad categories, all of them involving the issue of physical force and the protection of men's rights: *the police*, to protect men from criminals – *the armed services*, to protect men from foreign invaders – *the law courts*, to settle disputes among men according to objective laws.

* Freedom is what "the haves" have. And freedom is what "the have-nots" have not.

QUOTATIONS FROM OTHER THINKERS ABOUT POLITICS AND LIBERTY

* Socialism means slavery. –Lord Acton

* No man is good enough to govern another man without his consent. –Abraham Lincoln

* What then is freedom? The power to live as one wishes. –Marcus Tullius Cicero

* Freedom is the emancipation from the arbitrary rule of other men. –Mortimer Adler

* Freedom is not a gift bestowed upon us by other men, but a right that belongs to us by the laws of...nature. –Benjamin Franklin

* Authority that does not exist for Liberty is not authority but force. –Lord Acton

* The rights of every man are diminished when the rights of one man are threatened. –John F. Kennedy

* The burden on the Federal Government has grown with great rapidity....The lessons of history, confirmed by the evidence immediately before me, show conclusively that continued dependence upon [government] relief induces a spiritual disintegration fundamentally destructive to the national fiber. To dole our relief in this way is to administer a narcotic, a subtle destroyer of the human spirit. It is inimical to the dictates of a sound policy. It is in violation of the traditions of America....The Federal Government must and shall quit this business of relief. –Franklin Roosevelt

* Let every nation know, whether it wishes us well or ill, that we shall pay any price, bear any burden, meet any hardship, support any friend, oppose any foe to assure the survival and the success of liberty. –John F. Kennedy

* I prefer dangerous freedom over peaceful slavery. –Thomas

Jefferson

* That government is best which governs the least, because its people discipline themselves. –Henry David Thoreau

* Life without liberty is like a body without spirit. –Kahlil Gibran

* Is is slavery, not to speak one's thought. –Euripides

* Live free or die: Death is not the worst of evils. –John Stark

* Slavery is the next thing to hell. –Harriet Tubman

* You get your freedom by letting your enemy know that you'll do anything to get it. Then you'll get it. It's the only way you'll get it. – Malcolm X

* Who would be free themselves must strike the blow. Better even to die free than to live slaves. –Frederick Douglass

* Disobedience is the true foundation of liberty. The obedient must be slaves. –Henry David Thoreau

* Those who expect to reap the blessings of freedom, must, like men, undergo the fatigue of supporting it. –Thomas Paine

* If you put a chain around the neck of a slave, the other end fastens itself around your own. –Ralph Waldo Emerson

* Find out just what any people will quietly submit to and you have the exact measure of the injustice and wrong which will be imposed on them. –Frederick Douglass

* The best government is that which teaches us to govern ourselves. –Johann Wolfgang von Goethe

* Most people want security in this world, not liberty. –H.L. Mencken

* No man can put a chain about the ankle of his fellow man without at last finding the other end fastened about his own neck. – Frederick Douglass

* Is freedom anything else than the right to live as we wish? Nothing else. –Epictetus

* A society that puts equality before freedom will get neither. A society that puts freedom before equality will get a high degree of both. –Milton Friedman

* None are more hopelessly enslaved than those who falsely believe they are free. –Johann Wolfgang von Goethe

* Your freedom is a supreme value. Nothing is higher than that. – Bhagwan Rajneesh

* The individual has always had to struggle to keep from being overwhelmed by the tribe. If you try it, you will be lonely often, and sometimes frightened. But no price is too high to pay for the privilege of owning yourself. –Friedrich Nietzsche

* In the end, [the ancient Romans] wanted security more than they wanted freedom. –Edward Gibbon

* I did not wish to live in a country where the individual does not enjoy equality before the law and freedom to say and teach what he likes. –Albert Einstein

* If liberty means anything at all, it means the right to tell people what they do not want to hear. –George Orwell

* My definition of a free society is a society where it is safe to be unpopular. –Adlai Stevenson

* If freedom of speech is taken away, then dumb and silent we may be led, like sheep to the slaughter. –George Washington

* The only valid censorship of ideas is the right of people not to listen. –Tom Smothers

* Think for yourselves and let others enjoy the privilege to do so, too. –Voltaire

* If we don't believe in freedom of expression for people we despise, we don't believe in it at all. –Noam Chomsky

* Freedom is always and exclusively freedom for the one who thinks differently. –Rosa Luxemburg

* The end of law is not to abolish or restrain, but to preserve and enlarge freedom. For in all the states of created beings capable of law, where there is no law, there is no freedom. –John Locke

* The liberties of our country, the freedoms of our civil Constitution are worth defending at all hazards; it is our duty to defend them against all attacks. –Samuel Adams

* Liberty has never come from the government. Liberty has always come from the subjects of it. The history of liberty is a history of resistance. –Woodrow Wilson

* No power on earth has a right to take our property from us without our consent. –John Jay

* It does not take a majority to prevail, but rather an irate, tireless minority, keen on setting brushfires of freedom in the minds of men. –Samuel Adams

FOR FURTHER READING

None of these books is necessary. If you read this book with any kind of intelligence, then you already understand everything important about politics. Still, if you want to expand your knowledge, or get a different viewpoint, these are the best books I know.

* *Economics in One Lesson* by Henry Hazlitt (1946, revised 1978). Much more interesting and exciting than the title suggests.

* *Capitalism: The Unknown Ideal* by Ayn Rand (1966). Ferocious guide to liberty by the greatest political innovator and expert ever.

* *The Revolution: A Manifesto* by Ron Paul (2008). Remarkably concise and yet profound.

* *Capitalism* by George Reisman (1996). Magisterial work of scholarship.

SPECIAL AUTHOR'S NOTE

Thank you for reading my book! If you wish to help the noble cause of political liberty and human freedom, please post a book review to Amazon.com or elsewhere. It need not be long! Just one or two sentences giving your honest opinion is great.

This will help world freedom tremendously. Far more than most people realize, book reviews enhance author prestige and future sales. If you add your voice to mine, people will notice and individual liberty will soar!

You can also send me your views of this book privately – however negative or positive. I'd like to hear them. It's very possible for me to improve this work for future editions. I'll try to respond respectfully to every thoughtful, insightful, or substantive comment.

Many thanks for your contributions to individual liberty and life on this earth!

Kyrel Zantonavitch
KyrelZ@gmx.com

Made in the USA
Middletown, DE
15 November 2021